Original title:
Life's Meaning… or Is It Just a Cosmic Prank?

Copyright © 2025 Creative Arts Management OÜ
All rights reserved.

Author: Colin Leclair
ISBN HARDBACK: 978-1-80566-140-5
ISBN PAPERBACK: 978-1-80566-435-2

Tales of Twisted Fates

In shadows where the plot does twist,
We dance on dreams that can't exist.
A jester's cap upon our heads,
We laugh as logic lightly treads.

Fortune flirts with a wink or two,
An ancient tale that feels brand new.
With cosmic giggles guiding fate,
We question, jest, and contemplate.

The Art of Existential Play

In the theater of the absurd,
We juggle thoughts that feel unheard.
With punchlines hidden in the stars,
We leap from hopes to dreams of Mars.

Each moment blooms with silly grace,
We twirl with absence in this space.
An actor's quip, a puppet's string,
In this grand mess, we dance and sing.

A Bizarre Balancing Act

On tightropes spun from whimsy's thread,
We sway between the wise and wed.
A circus clown in cosmic jest,
We tiptoe past the silly quest.

With every wobble, laughter reigns,
As we search for joy amidst the pains.
The universe winks in mischief's light,
And we chuckle through the starry night.

The Cosmic Scavenger Hunt

We scour stars for clues of fate,
In galactic nooks, we navigate.
A feather here, a marble there,
Collecting laughs — we're quite a pair.

The map is scribbled with rogue delight,
As comets giggle, shining bright.
In absurd puzzles we entwine,
Unraveling jokes as we align.

Shadows of Laughter in the Void

In shadows dark, we find our cheer,
Where echoes dance, both far and near.
A cosmic joke, we laugh and sigh,
Floating on whims, we wonder why.

Stars above play peek-a-boo,
While planets swirl, creating a stew.
Tickling fate with every choice,
In silence, we hear the universe's voice.

The Paradox of Purpose

With purpose clear, yet blurred the lines,
We search for answers in grapevine signs.
A buffet of dreams, we take a seat,
Sampling chaos, it's quite a treat!

Jesters in robes, parading around,
They juggle our hopes, oh, what a sound!
Each twist and turn, a giggling fate,
Unraveling threads, we can't sedate.

Scribbles on the Canvas of Existence

Life's a canvas, scribbled in haste,
Colors collide, none go to waste.
Crayons drop from chubby hands,
While giggles burst like marching bands.

Each stroke a question, wild and free,
A doodle of thoughts, come play with me.
In the gallery of forgotten dreams,
We marvel at laughter, bursting at seams.

Whims of the Celestial Jester

A jester spins the cosmos round,
Tickling stars without a sound.
His laugh fills space, a comet's tail,
As he hurls fate without fail.

With rubber chickens, he shakes the sky,
While we all ponder, "Oh, my, oh my!"
The punches land, but we still grin,
For in this jest, it seems we win.

An Exploration of Wonderment

In a world of spinning stars, we laugh,
Chasing dreams like butterflies, oh what a gaffe.
Sock puppets debate the cosmos at night,
With wigs and capes, they aim for delight.

Sipping tea with raccoons in a tree,
They speak of taxes and global glee.
Noses twitching, they hold a debate,
Over how the moon is a giant plate.

A fish once claimed it swam through a book,
Telling tales of monsters, come take a look!
While pencils stretch and erasers fly,
We ponder why pizzas don't always try.

In gardens where time plots chaos and cheer,
Sunflowers freestyle, showing no fear.
While ants form a band, boogying away,
We giggle at truths in a cosmic ballet.

So dance like the wind, and sing like the rain,
Paint sunny smiles on a canvas of pain.
For in this riddle, funny and bold,
We find our essence, our stories unfold.

A Symphony of Serendipity

In the morning, socks lost fame,
A tango with the dryer, what a game!
Coffee spills like laughter's tune,
Chasing thoughts that float like balloons.

Frogs wear crowns in the afternoon,
Dancing under a silver moon.
A cat's meow sings a tune divine,
As we question our design.

Bearings on the Unknown

Maps scribbled in crayon line,
Every turn a grand design.
With compass turned to true absurd,
Lost and found among the herd.

A swing on Neptune, round the sun,
Chasing dreams, oh what fun!
Tangled thoughts like shoelaces,
In the dance of cosmic races.

Nonsense in the Grand Scheme

The stars giggle and wink with glee,
As we ponder what's meant to be.
A pickle jar holds ancient fate,
Pickles laughing while we wait.

Clouds wear hats, and rain falls up,
Reality tastes like a fizzy cup.
Chasing shadows with a spoon,
In this jester's afternoon.

Chronicles of Cosmic Curiosity

Planets trade their secrets bold,
In cosmic whispers, they unfold.
A wormhole's dance, a silly spree,
As time giggles in jubilee.

Whys and hows in random jest,
Roaming thoughts, an endless quest.
With quirks and quirks, we spin and sway,
In this outrageous cabaret.

Puzzles of Existence

What's the point of chasing stars?
When we're tripping over jars.
Each question twists in a knot,
As answers dance in a pot.

A hamster wheel that spins for fun,
Racing hard, but we're not done.
The universe plays hide and seek,
With every truth that feels quite weak.

A cat's meow in the silence cries,
Whiskers twitching with knowing eyes.
Are we pawns in a grand design?
Or just the jesters' lunch, divine?

We coin our thoughts like silly jokes,
While destiny chuckles, then pokes.
In every riddle, we learn to grin,
For laughter's the best medicine within.

The Canvas of Confusion

A brush of fate, a splash of hue,
We paint our lives, but sketch askew.
What's bright today may dull tomorrow,
Yet we dive right in with no sorrow.

Colors blend in puzzling ways,
Like socks lost in the washing maze.
Every scribble tells a tale,
Of grand designs that often fail.

The canvas stretches far and wide,
Filled with chaos we cannot hide.
Shapes and forms, a jumbled mix,
In this gallery of cosmic tricks.

Amidst the mess, joy can be found,
In every splash, absurd and profound.
We step back and give a cheer,
For art's just life wearing silly gear.

Fragments of a Cosmic Joke

In the silence of the starlit night,
Do shadows giggle at our plight?
As we ponder what's the score,
The cosmos laughs and asks for more.

A cosmic pun, a warped delight,
As we search for sense in the twilight.
Every stumble, a punchline tossed,
In the grand theater where logic's lost.

We dance like marionettes on strings,
Chasing meaning while chaos sings.
With each misstep that we make,
The universe grins, a big ol' flake.

Fragments scattered, like confetti bright,
Filling our hearts with sheer delight.
We're all players in this grand scheme,
Sipping laughter while we dream.

Searching for Signs in the Dark

Beneath the moonlight's playful glare,
We seek our truths in the cool night air.
With maps and clues that lead us astray,
While the stars simply laugh at our fray.

An arrow points but doesn't stay,
Guiding us down a ridiculous way.
We squint our eyes for a glimpse of sense,
But find only riddles that leave us tense.

Navigating through cosmic signs,
Where every path is filled with lines.
Do we follow shadows or chase the light?
Or are we just fumbling in the night?

In our search for answers and clues,
The universe winks, plays coy with dues.
And in this game of hide and seek,
We chuckle softly, for we are unique.

Existential Whispers

In shadows deep, we ponder fate,
A cosmic giggle, oh, isn't it great?
Stars twinkle down with a cheeky wink,
As we sip coffee and spill our drink.

Questions swirl like leaves in the breeze,
Are we but marionettes with no keys?
The universe laughs; it's all just a game,
And here we are, fumbling the same.

The Universe's Playful Jest

Galaxies swirl in an endless spin,
While we chase our tails with a lopsided grin.
What's this all for? A grand cosmic show?
Or just a big joke that we don't quite know?

Maybe it's all in a puppet's hand,
Pulling the strings while we misunderstand.
With every question, the laughter grows,
Tickled by fate as the mystery flows.

Echoes of a Celestial Joke

Comets dash past with a wink and nod,
As we trudge through life, occasionally flawed.
Silly debates on the grand design,
Yet the stars just giggle with sparkling wine.

Philosophers ponder, thinkers all frown,
While the cosmos dances, up and down.
In the midst of chaos, a joke is spun,
As we chase shadows, missing the fun.

When Infinity Smirks

Time ticks on, with a sly little grin,
Playing hide and seek as it draws us in.
We build our castles on sand and on dreams,
While the universe chuckles at our schemes.

Endless cycles, like a carnival ride,
Around and around, nowhere to hide.
But in the whirl, joy often brings,
A glimpse of wisdom in silly things.

The Philosophy of Absurdity

In a world where socks go missing,
I ponder all the points I'm missing.
The universe just winks and grins,
As I trip over my shoelace spins.

Cats in hats and dogs that dance,
Whisked away in happenstance.
Jupiter's laughing, can't you see?
Twirling around on a cosmic spree.

Pickles in a jar with glee,
In a land of what could never be.
Marshmallow clouds and chocolate streams,
Silly and sweet in all our dreams.

Absurdity reigns with style and flair,
Even when I forget my hair.
A dance of nonsense, a riddle, a game,
Laughter heralds the absurdity's fame.

Journey Through Quixotic Realms

On a quest for a grail made of crumpets,
With knights who ride on tricycles' bumpets.
I chased a mirage of grand delusion,
In a kaleidoscope of confounding fusion.

Unicorns sipping tea in the park,
While jellybeans sing with a chirpy lark.
My quest for truth leads to bubblegum,
In a land where serious thoughts just succumb.

Every corner I turn—what a sight!
Giraffes in pajamas, oh what delight!
Building castles from cotton candy dreams,
Finding wisdom in giggles and memes.

So let's frolic through this whimsical space,
With laughter as our only grace.
No sense to be made, but oh what fun,
As we twirl in the glow of the candy sun.

Nods from the Cosmos

Stars are just winking in greeting,
As I ponder what's worth competing.
The moon snickers at my tea cup spills,
A cosmic giggle amid the spills.

Planets juggle in a grand parade,
While meteors throw confetti and invade.
What wisdom lies in these wild whims?
It's a riddle wrapped in a cosmic hymn.

Black holes that burp like great old men,
Chasing dreams through the cosmic den.
Time wriggles like a worm on the hook,
Scribbling laughs in every nook.

So let's toast with a fizzy drink,
To the stars that nod and make us think.
In this vastness, laughter is our creed,
Waltzing through space with cosmic speed.

The Master of Ceremonies

Here stands the jester, hat askew,
With a scepter made of leftover glue.
Today's agenda: absurdity reigns,
Stringing together our silliness chains.

Welcome, welcome, all to the show,
Where rhythms stumble and ideas flow.
A rock that rolls, a cat that sings,
Watch as the universe flaps its wings.

Cactus dancers on stage tonight,
Hilarity blooms in the spotlight's light.
The punchline lands like a clumsy toe,
Tickling the cosmos, ready to go.

With laughter as our grand esprit,
We'll juggle the stars, wild and free.
In this circus of chaos, take a seat,
Life's a jest, and it's quite the treat!

Scripting the Unscripted

In a world of chance and jest,
Scripts are written, but not the best.
We dance through fate in silly shoes,
Laughing off the cosmic blues.

A plot twist here, a giggle there,
Life's a stage, but who's aware?
Characters, they come and go,
Punchlines land, and off we flow.

With cue cards held by stars above,
We improvise on paths of love.
Jokes fall flat, but smiles arise,
In playful chaos, wisdom lies.

So let's toast to the absurd,
To the cosmic script, so often blurred.
In this theater of the strange,
We find our joy in every change.

Whimsy from the Void

From emptiness, a chuckle flies,
As galaxies spin in goofy ties.
The void, it winks, with cosmic glee,
While stars throw shade, quite playfully.

A comet trips on stardust trails,
While planets giggle, sharing tales.
What's profound is often odd,
In this grand show, we give a nod.

So let's embrace this cosmic joke,
For in the mischief, wisdom pokes.
In every glance at skies so wide,
Lies whimsy mixed with endless pride.

We chuckle at our fleeting fate,
As shadows dance with love and hate.
With laughter echoing through the dark,
We twirl along, a cosmic spark.

Moments of Cosmic Clarity

In fleeting flashes, truth appears,
Amidst the laughter, joy, and tears.
A wink from fate, a silly twist,
Reveals the things we often missed.

A cosmic dance of highs and lows,
In awkward twirls, our spirit grows.
Moments spark with vibrant light,
As chaos bends the rules of night.

Questions swirl like stars above,
In playful banter, skies we love.
The universe teases with a smirk,
In every quirk, a cosmic work.

When clarity strikes with a cosmic grin,
We laugh aloud, let the day begin.
In this delicate balance, we reside,
With truth and humor as our guide.

The Playful Paradox

In life's absurdity, we find delight,
A paradox that feels so right.
With questions buzzing like a bee,
What's serious here? It's hard to see.

The sun wears shades in utter bliss,
As shadows play at cosmic risk.
We juggle answers, toss them high,
While laughter echoes through the sky.

With every problem, humor blooms,
In crowded hearts, the giggle looms.
We chase the light, we chase the fun,
In playful antics, we all run.

So here's to all the winks of fate,
And every friend who shared a plate.
In this paradox, let's take a chance,
And join the universe in its dance.

The Silly Thread of Cosmic Connection

In the fabric of space we weave,
Strange patterns that make us grieve.
A twist of fate, a silly yarn,
Pulls us closer, yet leaves us torn.

Stars giggle as they collide,
Dancing on a cosmic slide.
Gravity's pull a playful tease,
Floating dreams on a gentle breeze.

Planets wobble in a jest,
As we search for our quest.
Twirling to a tune we can't hear,
With every step, we persevere.

In the end, a laughing face,
Mocks our frantic, awkward race.
Unraveled threads, oh what a sight,
For in folly, we find delight.

The Grin in the Infinity Mirror.

Gazing deep into the glass,
Reflecting worlds that swiftly pass.
A wink from fate, a chuckle bright,
Infinity holds no end in sight.

Reflections stretch, absurd and wise,
Showing life in silly guise.
A mime's performance, cosmic show,
In every echo, laughter flows.

We chase the spark, yet miss the cue,
In endless loops, like déjà vu.
The punchline hides in plain old sight,
A fleeting grin, a cosmic bite.

Behind the veil, the jesters play,
Tossing truths in a childish way.
So let us laugh, and dance around,
For joy's the secret to be found.

Whispers of Purpose

In shadows deep, whispers arise,
Filled with secrets and sly surprise.
Questions tumble like marbles down,
Where is purpose, wearing a crown?

A squirrel sits, plotting its schemes,
While we ponder on faded dreams.
Tiny marches, great charades,
Life's silly game, in shades and fades.

Blowing bubbles, oh so grand,
Like beach balls tossed by unseen hand.
Silly clues scattered about,
Laughter's echo, no room for doubt.

In jest we find a path so bright,
In chaos too, there gleams a light.
For in the whispers, laughter's heat,
A purpose found, though it's bittersweet.

The Jester's Riddle

An old jester chuckles with glee,
Asking riddles, just wait and see.
A question spins with wobbly grace,
What's the meaning in our race?

He juggles stars, a plate of cheese,
With every toss, the universe flees.
A riddle wrapped in cosmic jest,
Are we simply jesters, at our best?

Laughing madly in a cartwheel's flight,
What's truth or folly in the night?
He leans in close, a wink to share,
"Life's just a game, if you dare!"

So spin and twirl, embrace the play,
In every misstep, find your way.
For in this riddle, you will see,
The greatest joke is simply… free.

Questing for Clarity in Confusion

In a maze of thoughts, I roam,
Each corner whispers, 'Welcome Home!'
I chase my tail in circles round,
While laughing at the lost I found.

With maps that lead to nowhere fast,
I ponder questions from the past.
Is there a guide in cosmic jest?
Or just a clown who loves this quest?

I wade through puddles of cloudy dreams,
Sprinkling stardust on gilded beams.
The answers twirl like fireflies bright,
Dancing just out of reach at night.

So here's to confusion, my dear friend,
With you, the fun never seems to end.
We'll toast to questions, raise a cheer,
For clarity may never appear!

When Questions Become Quirks

Why do ducks quack in sync, my friend?
Is that a message we should send?
With every thought, I tumble down,
Into the rabbit hole of my crown.

Curly mustaches on bewildered goats,
Pondering life's odd little notes.
Each whimsy wrapped in cosmic glee,
Makes me question what's, 'meant to be.'

There's joy in quirks that curl the lip,
Like jolly turtles doing the dip.
If laughing's wrong, then I don't want right,
As I embrace this silliness bright!

So let's invite the bizarre to play,
In a world painted shades of gray.
With every chuckle under the sun,
I find a twist—each question's fun!

Serene Chaos Under Starry Skies

Under stars, I sip cosmic tea,
Wondering if this is all for me.
Planets wobble in their old dance,
While I giggle at fate's strange romance.

Comets collide with raucous glee,
A waltz of chaos, pure and free.
In serene madness, I paint my fate,
With wonder sprinkled before it's late.

The universe chuckles, sly and fat,
As I chase after a flying cat.
Stars wink down with mischievous flair,
Whispering secrets that hang in air.

So I'll dance in this cosmic stew,
With hearts that sparkle and skies of blue.
For in chaos, there's joy to be found,
In the laughter of stars, all around.

Navigating the Absurd Aisles of Reality

I stroll through aisles of quirky sights,
Where socks and spoons hold lively fights.
Each shelf lined with whimsical dreams,
Echoing laughter in peculiar themes.

Tangled thoughts make for tangled ways,
Guiding me through absurd displays.
Should I buy a thought or a smile?
Which aisle holds wisdom worth my while?

Beyond each corner lies surprise,
Like a dancing cow in polka ties.
Reality's a playful jest,
In this store of odd choices, I'm blessed.

So I'll take my cart, let whimsy steer,
For navigating joy is crystal clear.
In aisles of absurd, I'll gladly play,
Collecting laughter, come what may!

Winks from the Abyss

Stars twinkle like they know a joke,
While planets dance, barely spoke.
The universe chuckles with glee,
As we wonder, 'What could this be?'

Laughter echoes in black holes deep,
Where secrets hide and shadows creep.
Do we orbit round reason or jest?
Sometimes the absurd feels like the best.

Galaxies swirl in a cosmic show,
Creating chaos with a wink, you know.
We're the audience, popcorn in hand,
Lost in the grandeur but not in command.

So here's to the jokes that the cosmos spins,
In this grand stage where the absurd begins.
With every twist and every turn,
We laugh at the fate that we didn't earn.

When Fate Plays Tricks

Fate's a joker with a deck of cards,
Dealing out surprises, often with regards.
Laughter mixed with a hint of dread,
Oh, what was that? The universe said!

Caught in a game of make-believe,
As we strive hard to achieve.
But like a kitten in a chrome tree,
Fate grins wide, saying, 'Just be free!'

We stumble and fall, we trip and spin,
As fate rolls dice with a mischievous grin.
With every change, we chuckle and sigh,
Playing along, it's a wild ride, oh my!

So here's to the messiness we embrace,
A dance of chaos in life's strange place.
When fate pulls a prank and laughs in delight,
We join in the laughter, hearts feeling light.

The Grand Design or Divine Comedy

A master plan or a grand façade?
Who writes the script, oh that's the charade!
We bumble along, a troupe gone astray,
With comedy gold in the games we play.

Cosmic puppeteers, tugging our strings,
Shooting confetti and other odd things.
Is it brilliance or goof? We're not quite sure,
Yet here we are, wanting more!

Life's a stage where the absurd shines bright,
We're characters lost in day and night.
Do we laugh or cry at the role we take?
With every mishap, new wonders awake!

So let's raise a glass to the cosmic jest,
In this divine dance, let's be the best.
For even if we don't know the play,
We'll laugh 'til the end—come what may!

Tales from the Infinite

In the infinity loop of what we call space,
We tumble through tales, at a dizzying pace.
Who wrote the script of our cosmic fate?
Just a prankster with a sense of great weight!

Time flips by like a cartoon reel,
Bending our thoughts, what a weird deal!
Each moment a sketch that tickles the mind,
Where punchlines hide and echoes unwind.

We're the punchlines in an endless joke,
Each smile and tear at fate's gentle poke.
Do we take it to heart or laugh with our soul?
For in this vast tale, we play the whole role!

So here's to the stories, the strange and the grim,
In the grand comic saga, let's all leap and swim.
With laughter as our guide and whimsy as our steer,
We create the tales that we hold dear.

Seeker of the Sublime

I wandered through the fields of thought,
Chasing dreams that laughter wrought.
With every step, I tripped on fate,
Giggling at the cosmic slate.

The sun winked down with a cheeky grin,
While shadows danced, keen to join in.
A question floated, quite absurd,
Do jellybeans hold truth, or just curds?

In a land where logic takes a break,
And reason stumbles for humor's sake.
I chased the wise, but they just laughed,
In the punchline of this absurd draft.

So, here I stand, on whimsy's edge,
Pondering boldly, on my own wedge.
Is the meaning here, or just a jest?
I'll keep on laughing; I think it's best.

When Stars Speak in Jest

The cosmos twinkled with a chuckle clear,
As planets pirouetted without any fear.
Comets zipped past with a silly shout,
While black holes whispered, "We're in doubt!"

Asteroids rolled like a cosmic band,
Playing tunes across the starlit land.
Galaxies winked in a dance so grand,
Is this a party, or just unplanned?

With moonbeams tickling the midnight air,
I laughed aloud without a care.
For every star that glimmers and beams,
Is just a reflection of our wild dreams.

So when stars speak, you hear the fun,
Echoes of laughter, their race just begun.
In this vast circus, we play our part,
Finding absurdity in every heart.

The Floating Castle of Illusions

Up in the sky, on clouds of fluff,
Stands a castle made of joke-stuffed stuff.
Its towers lean with a comic grace,
A wobbly world of giggles and space.

The doors swing wide and the laughter flows,
Inside are dreams in mismatched clothes.
Where the prince trips on banana peels,
And everything twists, just like our reels.

To see the queen with a crown of pies,
Ruling the jest with twinkling eyes.
Knights jousting with rubber duck shields,
In this realm where laughter yields.

Flying high on snickers and grins,
This floating castle of wild whims.
Here every turn leads to a prank,
And purpose drifts in a humorous bank.

Cosmic Queries

What if the stars play hide and seek?
And the planets giggle when we peek?
Are black holes just portals for jest,
Or cosmic mailboxes with humor expressed?

Does time ever trip on its shoelace threads,
While spacetime stretches, rolling its heads?
Are we the punchlines in a universal joke,
Just puppets dancing, or wise blokes?

A comet could be simply a flung pie,
While gravity whispers, 'Oh my, oh my!'
And in every moment, do we just pause?
To ponder our fate, or laugh without cause?

So let's raise a glass, or perhaps a toast,
To the silly riddles that we love most.
For in this vastness, what can we find?
Just a playful prank, to tease the mind.

Reflections in a Cosmic Funhouse

In mirrors warped, we start to grin,
A universe full of cosmic sins.
The planets giggle, the stars make faces,
Reality's just a series of chases.

We trip on comets, slide on moons,
Play hopscotch with elusive tunes.
Galaxies whirl in a jolly spree,
Who needs answers with such hilarity?

Black holes sucking our thoughtful bits,
While aliens laugh at our silly skits.
Is there a guide to this zany ride?
Or just a clown with a cosmic slide?

The Riddle of Stars Unfolding

Stars play hide and seek at night,
While we ponder our cosmic plight.
Gravity giggles as we drift and sway,
In the universe's grand cabaret.

With each twinkle, a joke is shared,
Why are we here? Who really cared?
The planets spin with a cheeky grin,
Saying, 'Join us, let the fun begin!'

Asteroids bounce in a comical dance,
As if they were caught in a trance.
In this bizarre celestial play,
What's the punchline? We just can't say!

The Dance of Serendipity

Serendipity leads with a wobbly step,
While the universe chuckles, and we inept.
A fluke of fate, or good fortune's whim,
We blink and stumble, the lights grow dim.

Chance encounters spin like a dream,
Filled with laughter and a playful gleam.
Fortune cookies, the cosmic delight,
Whispering secrets in the middle of night.

We fumble through puzzles, all upside down,
In this world where we wear a frown.
Yet amidst the chaos, what a thrill,
Serendipity shouts, 'You know the drill!'

Why Do We Chase the Elusive Light?

Chasing light like it's a game,
While shadows giggle and call our name.
The glow teases like a sly old fox,
Running circles 'round discovery blocks.

With each step closer, it fades away,
Leaving us baffled, in disarray.
So we tumble through the twilight glow,
Laughing at the cosmic show.

What's the point of this restless chase?
Are we players in a cheeky space?
In pursuit of truth, we spin and sway,
Lost in the moments that won't stay.

The Trickster's Touch

In the cosmic dance, stars play a game,
Juggling life with a wink, never the same.
We ask for a sign, they laugh from the sky,
'There's no manual, mate, just try to fly!'

Every twist and turn, a shove or a tease,
Fortunes written in the breeze.
We trip on fate as it snickers aloud,
Who knew the universe could be so proud?

Like a cat with a yarn, it pulls on our dreams,
Tangles our thoughts in mischievous schemes.
We chase after answers, but they roll away,
Just a cosmic jester, having its play.

When we think we know, it shifts and it sways,
The joke's on us in the grand masquerade.
So let's raise a glass to this whimsical ride,
With laughter our compass, let humor be our guide.

Dreams of a Stellar Imposition

Woke up today, I swear I was a star,
Zooming through the cosmos, but where's my car?
Planets in pajamas, they giggle and spin,
Trading earthly worries for a cosmic grin.

Clouds whisper secrets, but they're hard to hear,
'Why think deep thoughts? Just have some beer!'
Galaxies twinkle, but do they have plans?
Or simply roll dice with their starry hands?

Asteroids pass by wearing comical hats,
Bouncing through space, they're all acrobats.
Gravity's got jokes, pulling with glee,
Who knew the void could be so carefree?

So let's not fret over fate's twisted thread,
Embrace the absurd, let it dance in your head.
The universe giggles, with secrets to chase,
Join in the laughter, it's a stellar embrace.

The Meaning in Mayhem

Life's a circus, clowns everywhere,
Juggling our troubles without a care.
Balancing dreams on a tightrope above,
As chaos reigns, and we learn to love.

The sun takes a bow, the moon throws confetti,
Stars crowd around, feeling all warm and sweaty.
Riddles unfold like a magician's act,
With laughter the trick, and joy the pact.

Giraffe in a suit gives a wink as we frown,
While elephants trumpet, turning smiles upside down.
The meaning's a puzzle, scattered in rhyme,
Wrapped in a giggle, dancing through time.

So let's toast to the mess, the joy and the strife,
With a chuckle and cheer, here's to this ride!
We'll flip through the pages of our upside-down book,
For mayhem's the heart, if we dare take a look.

In Pursuit of the Unknowable

Chasing shadows in the dead of night,
Hoping for answers that stay out of sight.
Mysteries beckon with a wink and a nudge,
'Come play with the cosmos, don't you dare judge!'

We question existence like it owes us a fee,
While the universe chuckles, just sipping its tea.
It tumbles and tumbles, a cosmic surprise,
Dropping hints in riddles wrapped in goodbyes.

Exploring the depths of our curious minds,
Bumping into truths that feel more like blinds.
With every discovery, another clue hides,
As our laughter confounds where the wisdom abides.

So here's to the seekers, the jokers, the wise,
In a world turned wacky under dark, starlit skies.
We'll dance in the chaos, embrace what we find,
For in the unknown, our spirits unwind.

The Enchanted Labyrinth

In a maze of thoughts, I twirl and spin,
Wondering where the chuckles begin.
A rabbit waves, with a silly grin,
Whispers of secrets, tangled within.

A mirror laughs, reflecting my face,
"Are you lost, or just in the wrong place?"
A jester leaps, with a froggy pace,
In this garden of chaos, I find my grace.

A spiral staircase takes me to new heights,
With gnomes dancing round, under twinkling lights.
"Is this real, or do we have flights? "
The stars chuckle softly, with delight in sights.

I trip on sanity, or maybe I don't,
Finding joy in the riddles, on dreams I can flaunt.
As the labyrinth closes, I giggle and haunt,
In a cosmic prank, here's what I flaunt!

Whirlwinds of Wonder

A gust of wind whispers, let's dance a jig,
A tornado of laughter, it's not so big.
Round and round, like a playful pig,
In this whirlwind of whimsy, I lightly dig.

Clouds wear hats and spin like a top,
With sunshine grinning, ready to bop.
Rainbows pop up, they giggle and drop,
In this storm of joy, I just can't stop.

The sun winks brightly, "What's the big deal?"
"Just have some fun, let your heart feel!"
Nature's a carnival, come join the reel,
In whirlwinds of wonder, we all can steal.

Chasing the bubbles that float in the sky,
I giggle at stars that just like to fly.
In a dance of delight, I laugh and cry,
This playful riddle, oh my, oh my!

Notes from the Beyond

A tune floats down from the cosmic void,
A melody of mischief, never destroyed.
With notes of stardust, they can't be toyed,
In harmony's laughter, I'm quite overjoyed.

In every heartbeat, a rhythm unfolds,
Like fish in a pond, with tales to be told.
"Why are we here?" it gently scolds,
"Just play along, let the truth be bold!"

Echoes of giggles from galaxies afar,
Whispering wisdom from the Moon's sweet guitar.
Each strum brings questions, each note a bizarre,
In this symphony, we're all the real star.

Dancing to melodies, swaying with grace,
Caught up in the laughter, lost in the chase.
Every silly moment leaves a trace,
In this grand concert, we find our place.

Flickers of a Cosmic Candle

In the dark, a wick softly flickers bright,
Like the universe chuckling into the night.
Each flame whispers secrets, ready to ignite,
Our cosmic joke that sets hearts alight.

Oh, luminous dazzle, what do you know?
Is this all a stage? Just put on a show?
As shadows dance wildly, with candlelight flow,
I laugh at the thought, as curiosities grow.

The wax drips slowly, shaping a tale,
With each little drop, there's laughter we hail.
From intergalactic realms, through wind and sail,
In this cosmic game, we'll never grow pale.

So let's toast to this glow, this flickering light,
Where humor and wisdom take joyous flight.
In the grand tapestry, we find our delight,
In each little giggle, we sparkle so bright!

Treading Water in a Cosmic Seesaw

Bobbing up and down, it's quite a show,
Swirling through the stars, where do we go?
Chasing after answers like a dog with a tail,
Wondering if humor's hidden in the ale.

Juggling with fate in a bright colored sphere,
Tickled by the cosmos, do we dare to cheer?
This floaty life might be a cosmic joke,
Or maybe just a prank played by a star-studded bloke.

Dancing on the waves, we stumble and spin,
Stardust on our noses, where do we begin?
A wink from a galaxy, a sly little grin,
Here's to the chaos, let the fun begin!

So let's toast to the wondrous, the wild and the strange,
In this zany world, nothing's really out of range.
Floating through quirkiness, we giggle and sway,
Together in the cosmic ballet, come what may.

The Illusion of Grand Design

Blueprints of the universe scribbled in chalk,
Who held the pencil? Was it time for a walk?
Twists and turns in a spaghetti-like scheme,
Are we all just players in a whimsical dream?

Curly Q galaxies spinning away,
They're laughing at us as we plan our next play.
Complexity's easier when it looks like a game,
Yet, every round we circle, it feels mostly the same.

Stargazing with giggles, we ponder the view,
Is fate just a ripoff of yesterday's stew?
Letting go of certainty, we ride waves of absurd,
Finding humor in moments, it's pretty preferred.

So let's dance in the chaos, twirl in our fog,
Sipping on mystery, sitting on a log.
With laughter as our compass, we merrily roam,
In the grand illusion, we've finally found home.

Phenomena of Playfulness

Sunshine spills laughter, rolling in waves,
Every day's a circus filled with whimsical knaves.
Sprinkling joy like confetti from the sky,
Is this universe jesting? Oh my, oh my!

Bouncing along like a bouncy castle dream,
Chasing all the giggles, it's the ultimate scheme.
With rubbery planets and comets that bounce,
Is fun a universal law? We'll take a goodounce!

With sketches of silliness and cosmic tickles,
Are we just marionettes in a grand set of nickels?
Each wondered question fluffs up like a cloud,
Waving at the cosmos, we'll shout it aloud.

So let's whirl in the nonsense, embrace the absurd,
Feathers of laughter in every last word.
In the playground of stardust, we giggle and play,
Feeling the echoes of cheer every day.

Searching for Truth in a Mirage

Wanderers we are, through deserts of thought,
Chasing down answers, but oh, how they're fraught!
Mirages of wisdom twist in the heat,
Is knowledge just vapor? It can't be a feat!

On the quest for the essence, we stumble and fall,
With shadows of questions that beckon our call.
Each answer a riddle, each truth wears a mask,
Finding solace in humor—oh, what a task!

Through laughter and wonder, we peek through the haze,
Digging for treasures buried in the craze.
Maybe the truths are just silly old gags,
Packed in a suitcase, with colorful rags.

So let's pirouette through this mirage-filled quest,
With giggles as our guide, it's surely the best.
In the search for the real, we flutter and sway,
In a world full of whimsy, let's dance and play!

Cosmic Whimsy

Stars wink in the vast night,
Planets dance in their flight.
A cosmic joke, oh what a tease,
Tickling the universe with ease.

Time ticks on with a goofy grin,
Dancing moments, where do we begin?
Frogs croak wisdom, cats chase their tails,
In this circus, reason often fails.

Black holes snicker, pulling us near,
As we spin tales, sipping on beer.
Every comet's just a prankster's tail,
Leaving us to wonder, without a veil.

So let's laugh at the stars above,
In this grand joke, let's share the love.
For in the chaos, joy shall reside,
As we wobble and glide on this cosmic ride.

Threads of the Absurd

In the fabric of thought, we spin a yarn,
Stitching nonsense in shadows and barn.
We chase our tails and take a dime,
Wondering if it's all just whimsy in rhyme.

Socks in pairs get lost in the mix,
Like existential questions without their fix.
If the universe winks, do we just grin?
Or ponder our fate as we loosen our skin?

Aliens laugh as they sip their brew,
Watching us juggle what's false and what's true.
"Do they know?" we whisper, as pigeons take flight,
While cats plot domination under moonlight.

With each thread we pull, the fabric unravels,
In this tapestry strange, reason travels.
Yet we dance in the absurd, no need for a guide,
For humor's the road where our quirks can reside.

Questioning the Cosmic Code

Quesadillas fall from the sky, oh dear,
Are they signals or snacks? Let's make that clear!
In the grand code, do we find our way?
Or is it just pixels in a cosmic ballet?

Fish in suits debate over tea,
Do they understand what it means to be?
Or are they just players in a sitcom play,
Tripping on cosmic lines day after day?

Galaxies collide with a hug and a laugh,
Creating new worlds, taking a gaff.
If fate's a script, we flip the page,
Laughing at the blunders of this grand stage.

So let's question the cosmos, while munching on toast,
In this prankster's playground, we'll raise a toast.
For in every riddle, let us find cheer,
In the twisted, quirky tapestry here.

The Playwright of Existence

A jester writes on a cosmic stage,
Crafting mischief through each silly page.
With every setup, a punchline awaits,
As the actors stumble through time's heavy gates.

The moon takes a bow, the sun has its quips,
While planets laugh hard, clutching their hips.
Each comet a prop, each star a grin,
In this wild show of that which has been.

Rehearsals are chaos, the plot's often lost,
Yet laughter and joy come at no cost.
Sketches of fate dance under the light,
Winking at us through the day and the night.

So applaud the absurd, enjoy the bizarre,
In this play of existence, we're all the stars.
For the playwright's got tricks, we giggle and cheer,
In a world full of wonders, let's lose all our fear.

Unmasking the Infinite Joke

In a world where socks disappear,
The fridge hums a secret cheer.
Cats plot under the moonlit glow,
What do they know? We'll never know.

Balloons float like thoughts gone astray,
Did you feel that? It slipped away.
Pickles hold wisdom in their brine,
This pickle's truth is truly divine.

Discounted dreams at the corner store,
Life's just a laugh, not a bore.
With each tumble, a stumble's grace,
We trip through time at a crazy pace.

So lift your glass, toast the absurd,
To nonsense spoken but rarely heard.
In the chaos, find a glimmer bright,
Here's to the joke that feels so right!

Riddles of Reality

We chase our tails, a dizzying dance,
Life throws lemons, not given the chance.
With each riddle wrapped in a laugh,
We scribble answers, then lose the half.

Spaghetti nights and coffee spills,
The universe giggles, it gives us thrills.
Why do we search for meaning so deep?
A pie in the face, while we laugh and weep.

Riding the waves of a cosmic jest,
Every question we ask feels like a test.
Do the stars chuckle at our plight?
While we spin tales through the endless night.

So let's toast to the joy in the strange,
In this circus of chaos, we'll never change.
With a wink and a grin, we sway and slide,
In this wild charade, let's take it in stride!

The Benevolent Trickster

Peeking behind the curtain wide,
Life plays tricks, a whimsical ride.
With laughter echoing in each facade,
The trickster smiles, isn't it odd?

Banana peels on the path ahead,
Mocking our plans, oh, how we're led.
Yet in every stumble, a lesson gleams,
The universe winks, as we chase our dreams.

Jellybeans fall from clouds so high,
Who knew the sky had a sweet supply?
With each surprise, we learn and grow,
Every punchline's timing, oh, what a show!

So let's raise our mugs to the twist and turn,
In this gala of jest, there's so much to learn.
For in the end, every silly wink,
Hints at the truth if we stop to think!

Stardust Conversations

Beneath the stars, we ponder deep,
What do they know? Secrets to keep.
The galaxies chuckle, a cosmic choir,
As we dance on earth, fueled by desire.

Salt on the rim of a margarita glass,
Do they watch and laugh as we let time pass?
Glitter and chaos, our daily dose,
In stardust whispers, we learn to coast.

Conversations with shadows, a fleeting guest,
Our laughter's the melody, the very best.
With a twinkle of eyes, they playfully tease,
In this universe, it's laughter that frees.

So let's spin and sway, with hearts open wide,
Finding joy in the ride, let the giggles collide.
For in every corner, and in every sigh,
Awaits another joke, just waiting to fly!

Mysterious Laughter in the Cosmos

In the dark of space, a giggle gleams,
Stars crack jokes, or so it seems.
Planets spin in dizzying jest,
As comets race, they never rest.

Asteroids chuckle, they tumble and drift,
Black holes hide secrets, giving us a rift.
Aliens might snicker at our little plight,
As we ponder our place in the endless night.

Nebulas swirl with colors so bright,
Cosmic clowns dance, what a sight!
Gravity pulls not only on our hearts,
But on laughter that binds all the parts.

So lift your gaze to the vast unknown,
Where humor's stitched in every stone.
For in the void, we're not alone,
Just stars in a farcical throne.

A Journey Beyond the Ordinary

Once a traveler, I sought some sense,
Navigating life without a fence.
Through forests of doubt, across sands of time,
Each twist and turn was quite sublime.

A rabbit spoke, tiptoeing past,
With tales of futures and shadows cast.
He grinned and winked, 'It's all a show,
Join the circus, don't be slow!'

With butterflies laughing, I danced in the breeze,
Chasing the echoes, life played with ease.
Each moment a prank, a tickle and tease,
In this whimsical world, I found my peace.

So grab your hat, let's join the parade,
For the ordinary's just a masquerade.
In every step, a jest unfolds,
Through all the chaos, truth just molds.

Prisms of Perception

We wear our lenses—what a sight,
Filter out joy, and lose the light.
Through dazzling prisms, we squint and stare,
But does the truth really linger there?

Each thought a color, brilliant and bold,
Stories unravel as the days unfold.
We chase reflections, in puddles so sly,
While meaning winks from the corner of the eye.

A kaleidoscope whispers, 'Look over here!'
Dancing delights in the atmosphere.
Yet if we perceive just a jester's game,
What's real or imagined? Who's to blame?

So let's toss the filters, embrace the fun,
Life's a jest, and we're not yet done.
With laughter echoing, through all we try,
We'll catch the joy as the moments fly.

Unraveling the Fabric of Perception

In the loom of the universe, we weave our thread,
Stitching together the things we dread.
Patterns emerge, bizarre and grand,
As we twirl about in this cosmic band.

A sock puppet speaks, and we're all ears,
Telling tales wrapped in whimsical fears.
What's woven with love might fray with a laugh,
Yet still, we dance on this curious path.

Each strand a moment, holding tight,
Glimmers of truth in the fading light.
We tug at the edges, unraveling fate,
Find giggles and sighs in this strange state.

So snip a thread and see what falls,
A tangle of joy in the cosmic halls.
In this grand tapestry, don't forget to play,
For laughter is the fabric that colors our day.

The Mirage of Significance

We search for purpose in the stars,
While juggling dreams like bouncing cars.
With every question, laughter rings,
Are we just puppets tied to strings?

A fortune cookie whispers fate,
While time just dances, rather late.
We toast to meaning with our tea,
As the cosmic joke winks at me.

A philosopher trips on a thought,
In a maze of riddles we are caught.
We cherish wisdom like a hoax,
And laugh aloud at all the blokes.

So grab your hat, let's take a ride,
On this merry-go-round of pride.
We'll chuckle 'til we see the light,
And find the humor in our plight.

Chasing Shadows of Enlightenment

I chased the shadow of a sage,
But found a cat with a wise old page.
It purred and blinked, a cosmic tease,
In search of truth, just take it easy.

We ponder questions, big and small,
As butterflies dance at the wall.
With socks mismatched, we seek the goal,
Yet trip on words, oh how we stroll!

The gurus promise blissful ways,
But all I see are cloudy days.
A squirrel laughs above my head,
"Just follow crumbs," it seems to said.

So here we sit, with popcorn dreams,
Amidst the chaos, life redeems.
We twirl and spin, the night's a jest,
In pursuit of shadows, we find rest.

Holograms of the Human Heart

A heart that's holographically bright,
Reflects our hopes in the pale moonlight.
With every beat, a tiny jest,
Are we the punchline? Just a guest!

We dance on strings of fate's design,
Our foibles shaped like silly wine.
In every hug, a cosmic swirl,
Who knew existence was such a whirl?

As laughter echoes through the air,
We run through folly without a care.
Our dreams are bubblegum on strings,
Chewed and blown 'til laughter sings.

So to the beat of life's weird tune,
We spin like tops beneath the moon.
And maybe joy's the tales we weave,
In funny fates, we all believe.

Serenade of the Cosmic Clown

In the circus of existence, we perform,
With painted faces, we break the norm.
Our laughter's raucous, our joys collide,
As we juggle moments, how we glide!

The cosmic clown with a silly grin,
Trickles punchlines through thick and thin.
He winks at us, we play along,
In this grand show, we all belong.

With pie fights splattered on the wall,
We find our truth in each pratfall.
Our woes are just balloons that pop,
In the carnival of dreams, we'll hop!

So join the dance; let's spin and sway,
As stars and laughter light the way.
In the serenade of cosmic jest,
We'll find our home, we won't regress.

Dancing in the Void

In the dark, we sway and spin,
With stars above, let the fun begin.
Gravity's just a suggestion, they say,
As we twirl in space, lost in the play.

Floating thoughts drift, light as air,
Jokes of the cosmos, if you dare.
Fumbling with dreams, like socks in a dryer,
Who knew existence could be such a flyer?

Galaxies giggle, snickering bright,
As we trip and stumble, oh what a sight!
Planets chuckle, share cosmic memes,
Life's a circus, bursting at the seams.

So let's celebrate this absurd ballet,
With laughter and joy, come what may.
In the void where nonsense reigns,
We dance to the rhythm of funny refrains.

Echoes of the Unseen

In shadows cast by a lively sun,
Echoes whisper, 'Oh what fun!'
Chasing phantoms, we trip on air,
With every laugh, we shed our care.

Mirthful nudges from the great unknown,
Clap your hands; you're not alone!
Invisible friends are all around,
In the silliness, we are bound.

Hiding in corners, the punchlines creep,
While time flows in a giggling sweep.
Peeking through curtains, they giggle and tease,
With wisdom wrapped in cosmic cheese.

The puns are plenty, the irony thick,
In this grand play, take your pick.
For in the whispers, a joke we glean,
Echoes of laughter in the unseen.

Beneath the Surface of Existence

Diving deep, what will we find?
Fishy mysteries that tickle the mind.
With every bubble, a curious tease,
As the universe winks with ease.

Coral jokes in vibrant hues,
Seahorses giggle with little clues.
Beneath the waves, absurd and spry,
Where even the starfish knows how to fly!

Whirlpool of thoughts, swirling and bright,
Reality's dance under moonlight.
Every splash sparks a laugh so divine,
What's bizarre down here, feels just fine.

As we swim through the cosmic sea,
With each wave, we're merrily free.
In this silly world, we twirl and dive,
Where humor and wonder truly thrive.

The Universe's Laugh

With twinkling eyes, the heavens grin,
At mortals spinning, where to begin?
Stars erupt into giggling light,
While comets race, just for delight.

Twirling planets, a cosmic show,
Juggling orbits with a playful flow.
Asteroids chuckle on their lonesome ride,
As they whizz past all with cosmic pride.

Silly quarks dance, in a quantum spree,
Wiggling about like it's all for free.
Black holes snicker, pulling us near,
With every twist, they cheer and jeer.

So let's toast to the stars up high,
To the cosmic creatures who wink and sigh.
For in this jest, we find our spark,
Laughter resounding in the vast, dark.

Whirlwinds of Wistful Wonder

In the circus of dreams we blend,
Chasing shadows that never bend.
Pixies giggle as we trip and fall,
Spinning round like a cosmic ball.

Juggling thoughts that slip through hands,
Building castles in shifting sands.
Each whimsy wave a slippery slope,
Wearing socks that bring us hope.

Silly questions float in the air,
Who decided to part our hair?
Amidst this dance of chance and fate,
We wonder if it's really too late.

With every punchline, laughter swells,
In this universe of ringing bells.
So hold on tight to your glowing dreams,
It's all a joke, or so it seems.

The Absurdity of Starry Aspirations

Wishing on stars with a wink and a grin,
Hoping they know what's deep within.
Galaxies giggle, their secrets unfurl,
As we stumble through this quirky whirl.

Planets play tag, or so we believe,
While we're stuck here, just trying to weave.
Meteors dance, leaving trails like a tease,
Reminding us life's never at ease.

Dreams take flight on bubblegum wings,
Melting away like forgotten things.
It's a comedy, this stellar show,
As we twirl around in the cosmic flow.

With whimsical thoughts that drift like balloons,
Under the shadows of colorful moons.
So laugh at the heavens, sing out your jest,
For in this absurdity, we're all just guests.

The Baffling Gift of Awareness

A gentle nudge, then we're awake,
Realizing every step's a fake.
Thoughts bounce around like rubber balls,
Echoing laughter in these hallowed halls.

Why do we ponder the how and the why?
While ants march on, and the clouds drift by.
A gift wrapped tight with a riddle inside,
As the universe winks, it's hard to decide.

Searching for wisdom in the odd and absurd,
But languages twist like a drunken bird.
Is there a point to this spinning spree?
Perhaps the joke is on you and me.

With coffee in hand and a smirk on our face,
We tumble through time at a breakneck pace.
So revel in here, the now, the zest,
In this baffling dance, we're truly blessed.

Cosmic Clowns in a Silent Theater

In a grand hall where silence roams,
Enter the jesters from far-off homes.
Their painted smiles hide the grand scheme,
Winking at us, they pull at the dream.

Tiptoeing through the cosmic giggle,
With oversized shoes they dance and wiggle.
The universe chuckles, a slapstick delight,
As stars throw confetti, lighting the night.

Each slap on the back, an echoing cheer,
Fills the quiet with laughter we hear.
What's the punchline of this interlude?
Perhaps it's the choice to be light-hearted, not crude.

So savor each moment, let irony thrive,
In this silent show, we're endlessly alive.
A riddle wrapped in laughter's embrace,
With cosmic clowns, we've found our place.

Shadows of Truth

In the corner, where shadows play,
A whisper chuckles, 'It's just a day.'
The light bends low, a prankster's game,
Is this all real, or just the same?

Socks in the dryer, they vanish quick,
Like truths we search for, a cosmic trick.
We dance with questions, hands in the air,
Only to find the answers aren't there.

A cat on the porch watches us strive,
With a look that says, 'Do you even thrive?'
While we ponder the profound with frown,
That feline knows it's just another clown.

So let's toast to puzzling, to laughs and fun,
To the joys of confusion, we've only begun.
For every reason we think we see,
Might just be nature's own comedy.

A Game of Stars

Stars wink from their cosmic perch,
Playing hide and seek, a grand old lurch.
With constellations all jumbled and tossed,
Are we the players, or just a lost cost?

Planets spin tales as comets dash by,
While we wonder, give me a reason why!
The moon rolls her eyes with a knowing grin,
In this game of stars, does anyone win?

So we scribble our hopes on the night sky's page,
As if somehow that'll assuage our rage.
But the universe giggles, diamond dust swirls,
And we dance to the rhythm, in cosmic whirls.

Perhaps we're just pieces in a cosmic board,
Rolling the dice, while the universe snored.
In this grand game, it's plain to be seen,
That laughter's the prize, and we're all just keen.

Reflections in a Cosmic Mirror

In the mirror of stars, so shiny and bright,
What do we see? Just our own silly plight.
Faces of joy, and a few of despair,
All jumbled together, as if we don't care.

Time bends and twists like a rubber band,
The cosmos laughs, isn't life just grand?
With laughs in the echoes of space and time,
And humor is found in the serious rhyme.

Threads of existence weave a fine dance,
As we juggle existence, our own merry chance.
We ponder the depths, then slip on a shoe,
Suddenly laughing at troubles we brew.

The mirror reflects all our most wacky traits,
As stars shout join in and celebrate.
With every twinkle, it's clear, so divine,
That humor's the secret, the best punchline.

The Quest for Illusions

In search of the truth, we wander afar,
Chasing rainbows and wishing on stars.
But every answer leads us in miles,
To more silly questions, and curious smiles.

Maps of existence, they're scribbled and torn,
Leading to places where laughter is born.
Though the quest feels weighty, like lugging a stone,
We frolic through pathways, never alone.

With a jester's cap and a grin so wide,
We march down the road, not caring the tide.
For every illusion we chase with glee,
Turns into laughter, wild and free.

So let's dance with these questions, let's twirl and spin,
In the quest for illusions, the giggles begin.
And whether we find what we think we seek,
The joy of the journey makes our hearts peak.

Beneath the Starlit Farce

Beneath the stars, we trod in glee,
With hiccups and laughs, oh can it be?
A cosmic joke or a clumsy dance,
We spin and twirl in a clueless trance.

The moon winks slyly, the sun just grins,
Are we the puppets or just silly twins?
Galaxies giggle, they're having a blast,
While we fumble through, hoping it lasts.

What if we're players in some grand jest?
The universe chuckles, we never guessed.
We trip over clouds, bump into stars,
As laughter echoes from Jupiter to Mars.

So here's to our folly, a toast with a cheer,
In the theater of cosmos, we hold dear.
No scripts to follow, just dance and prance,
In this starlit farce, we take our chance.

Philosophies in a Cosmic Clown's Hat

In a jester's hat, thoughts spin around,
Truths wrapped in riddles, absurdly profound.
With rubber chickens and pies to the face,
We ponder the essence of this crazy place.

A giggle from Pluto, a snicker from Mars,
They whisper secrets, hidden in stars.
We juggle our worries, like a circus act,
Life's grand show, and there's no way to act!

Existential crises bounce like a ball,
What's the point if we're destined to fall?
Yet each tumble is met with a roar,
A reminder our follies are never a bore.

So gather your thoughts in that clown's funny hat,
To jest is divine, to ponder—how 'bout that?
For in laughter lies wisdom, wrapped tight like a gift,
In the circus of cosmos, it's the greatest gift.

Burdened by Cosmic Comedy

A cosmic comic, I toil and I jest,
With jokes that are odd and riddles at best.
Each day I awake with a chuckle or two,
What's on the agenda? A giggle or boo?

Planets collide in a slapstick parade,
As I question the roles my fortune has made.
Am I the punchline or just in on the game?
The more that I ponder, the more it feels the same.

With each twist and turn, hilarity grows,
As stars overhead do their comedic shows.
I trip on my thoughts, I trip on my feet,
Yet laughter rings louder, it feels like a treat!

So I embrace the funny, hold tight to the fun,
For in this vast circus, we all share the sun.
Though cosmic confusion may dance in my mind,
I'll embrace every giggle that I can find.

Dreams of a Witty Cosmos

In my dreams, there's a universe spinning,
Where wit is the coin and laughter's the winning.
Stars don't just shine, they wink with delight,
In the playground of night, everything feels right.

Meteors dance with a comical grace,
While black holes chuckle, losing their place.
Do planets conspire for a cosmic laugh?
Or is this all part of a galactic gaffe?

Comets race by, with tails full of glee,
As I dream of a cosmos eternally free.
With each silly twist of the universe's fate,
I find joy in every laugh, never too late.

So let's toast to the strange, the awkward, the bright,
In this grand cosmic joke, everything feels right.
For in laughter's embrace, we find our true spark,
In the dreams of the cosmos, we leave our mark.

www.ingramcontent.com/pod-product-compliance
Lightning Source LLC
Chambersburg PA
CBHW051637160426
43209CB00004B/688